Wife of Osiris
Meryl Pugh

VERVE
POETRY PRESS
BIRMINGHAM

PUBLISHED BY VERVE POETRY PRESS
https://vervepoetrypress.com
mail@vervepoetrypress.com

FIRST PUBLISHED MAY 2021

Printed and bound in the UK
by Positive Print, Birmingham

ISBN: 978-1-912565-60-3

November 2023

Wife of
Osiris

A field of flowered and seeding grasses, waist-high.

She is wearing red, he is wearing his gold aspect.

The seeds ascend, corona of light around each hard particle.
Then it's

the ground disappearing and day flicking to night each colour
to its opposite each object to its other side each being to its
other face

flecks of radiant everything coming loose and warm

His gift today: flight. She swoops above the city's river like a swallow – like, in fact, the birds around her: not swallows, small, with long tails, navy tufts either side of the head, the whole flock landing, now, on the water.

Then dark underneath, racing her shadow: a school of many large fish. One rises towards a little bird, opens its mouth. Good for the fish, she thinks, accepting the bird's death – but the bird twitches away. Good for the bird.

Her shadow picks up speed on the choppy grey shine as the school curves away. Then white spray, leaping: submarine, orca, goddess rising? Grey porpoises break surface – two columns proceeding in stately manner upstream.

Who has called such creatures? Who schools these wild things to such a showing? Not Osiris, absented again. For she has lost his gift, is coughing and paddling in their wake.

She curls into a booth in her fine dress; a band she loved three decades ago are playing. The wife of Osiris wants to see how far the singer's tattoos extend, twist the long hair around a wrist, but the singer is younger than she. Centuries.

*

She finds herself in socks – the wet of the cubicle floor seeping through – and she must go from attendant to supervisor to manager, asking about her shoes, but they can produce nothing that's her, poor substitutes only.

Who is she again? Just a person who can go below and return; activity forced upon her by circumstance. She is not, in herself, remarkable. In her allegiance she makes the waters to rise, she crosses rivers, she passes from day to night and back again.

She walks in light pyjamas through groups of people holding wine glasses, under arches, over paving, through lobbies and foyers and atria; she is looking for her street, her flat. The concert is about to begin, there are smiles, but she has gone the wrong way and feels stupid. She is not going to the concert.

The wife of Osiris is too bright and hard for this place, she bursts out through the double doors into the night, she begs her god's fire to come out of the sky and take her. But the street light is still the street light, the young glance nervously, there is no one here who wants her or who she wants. And her husband, who knew it would be this way, is still absent.

She surprises an intruder. She pushes the woman down on the floor, face against the radiator, hisses *He will come for you.*

*

If he does, it will be in glints and sideways glances.

She walks abroad, partakes of the world's riches as if under his instruction. That is, as if in his presence. Under his protection.

Inside the aura, her body contracts, her mass is greater, her texture denser. There is a moment of pause; everything is about to ascend. But in the singing exhalation that follows, she tips over into too-solid falling. She is weighted too quickly in this field of rising grass seed, floating pinpoints lit. She wants to raise her arms, be light, fingertips, sun, warmth.

She is still her own body sitting heavy between the stems.

Why does she wake with heart thump and trouble in mind?

You might as well ask the satellites in their swift congress with the earth, the hard, clear moon.

Metal struts from her mouth to the floor. Her jaw to be re-aligned. She feels no pain except a slight click elsewhere in her head. She may not speak.

She watches the officiant pronounce this, watches the pronouncement falter in the air, watches his transformation; he has grey skin now, he has studs along his jaw. He limps away, holding his face.

The struts release her. She feels no pain.

*

Two men attempt to gain entrance. But no, rose-pink, it is hers and they fall away, they are silt in the river, they did not hurt her.

There was a – not a wife exactly, but another, certainly – before. A god-sister who brought him back to life. Who made him a penis out of gold and bore him a child before he slipped back into the realm-of-every-moment. How can she compete with that? She cannot.

She tours the island coastline on a barge. It hovers above calm waters as they disembark. They squeeze between rocks – behind which is fire – as they take the path that crosses steep cliffs to reach the city. It is filthy and the residents acknowledge her disgust.

*

The wife of Osiris walks through official corridors with her host. They speak – such words – and pass beneath the arch, abreast.

What have they called down upon the blue-grey carpet, the rows of chairs, the institutional art? The woman in uniform beside her – who means so well, who wants to act all for the best – needs guidance and there is none.

Nothing accrues to the niche in the wall, the vase of peacock feathers. Nothing gathers in the air above the candle flame. Disaster is not halted, war is not averted. And she – the privileged – will not suffer.

What would it be like, to cast off his protection? To live like the woman beside her?

Inside the palace, white linen over a circular table.

A cat which cannot look away from its mirror image,
suspended in the air above it.

Her companion lacks the right clothes, splits in two, disappears.

*

Screaming wakes her; someone just out of view in dressing
gown and damage, a stripe of red down the front, red at the
neck.

She sits up. There is no one.

She is having sex with a war criminal. She knows he is a war criminal but she doesn't care. He lies on the ground, still in his fatigues, as she bares herself. Osiris' golden aura fills her eyes, clouds the air around them. The war criminal will not lean on her throat and snap her windpipe, he will not penetrate her anally against her will, he will not penetrate her orally against her will, he will not remove the condom without her knowledge, he will not call his friends. He will find his carefulness and patience as she takes her pleasure.

An interruption: roaring, howling, grating. Buckling metal, powdering brick. It lifts her away before they are finished and she passes (disappointment, thwart) through the bare woods, the pitted earth, the bombed houses as her husband causes the stars to wheel overhead. No matter. She will find a better occasion. She has time, all of it – more than the war criminal, who has been found by the children of his victims and is being torn, slowly, to shreds. Actual shreds.

Tonight, she takes her pleasure from the captives of the moment: doorways narrowing, shoulders gripped, no eye contact.

All the rooms in the house are open to her as she collects her clothes, steps around exploded corpses. Is she the cause? Her failure in the matter of averting war, her failure in the matter of his aura? How it wraps only her?

It doesn't matter. Death at some point is always certain.

She tells herself.

If she truly is the wife of Osiris, then the god has his attention on other things.

She dreamt, she remembers, the night she signed the contract. Something about a bathtub, something about a surgical saw.

She stares at the tunnel wall. The platform is deserted.

Something about her leg. If she takes a step, will it bear her weight? Rough barbs around her thigh, still fresh.

The thought presents itself: why not jump? As behind glass, she watches her feet. One step. The ceramic and metal objects that consist the tracks. But injury, pain (recoiling). One step backwards, then.

The thought remains like a concrete block hurled at her feet, external to her. The lights approach, the rails are gilded and hum. She gets on the train.

Afterwards, she enquires: Was it real?

Is her life real?

Summer in a city park. Sweet chestnut in full flower at noon smells savoury, like good, clean cock. Lime blossom is sweet like freesias, like jasmine, but with a citrus edge. She sipped her tisane and returned his gaze, those centuries ago. *Tilleul*, she said.

Now look.

Why her, and why this marriage?

All contracts need a premise.

(She can't blame him for not bothering any more. Things are very different these days.)

*

She is the necessary anchor. She is the aerial, she is the song, she is the ball of string, the trail of crumbs, the tree branch. She is the back-of-the-head that must never turn. Until he doesn't want to anymore.

Come back, that is. He might, at any time,

she tells herself.

Is this a dream? She is chasing someone down a curved
corridor, panelled in wood; someone who snatches at the walls,
making of them a stiff cape that loosens and softens into living
timber, leaf and bird, rain and guts and breath of beast. She is
shouting at the figure – and cannot call it back, too late, for the
quarry stops and turns, faces her, becomes

what?

Cape of red dilating into suns of red prisms, a flower of dazzle-
dimension-capacity, radiating frequencies not visible with
these eyes like a mandala like a

the god is silent

Is this a dream? An undulating field of links, each made of wood, spreading to the horizon, a red-orange line against the dark sky, reflected in the swaying surface drifting towards it. A link flips over, reveals its underside (always a face, no expression), flips back to its smooth reverse.

Standing on the edge above it, she raises her foot to board the drift-sea, let it bear her forward, steps

but the links just ripple, sag a little under her weight. She stands between brink and horizon. Nothing carries her forward.

This isn't what she thought it was – the End, or the lightened burden of the self. It is something else, shoddier.

There is still the matter of the faces on the underside of this rippling thing. The wrongness.

This time – when she leaves the white-gold egg of her room, shuts her door on the light that falls on her good furniture – she leaves the aura behind.

Greasy marks on the banisters. Missing kerbstones. A melted litter bin.

The world is suddenly loud again

and when a man spits in front of her, she knows her luck has changed.

F r e e

A b a n d o n e d

All the time she was his wife and looked for him in the storm of butterflies that threw themselves across her path, the bird of prey that held position over the carpark, the peacock on the wall of the ruined palace gardens, she was misdirected.

Is this a dream? She closes her eyes and the heat-heart of red flowering fills everything, blood of the flower that is everywhere, rose mandala of being, rose of great being working.

Wife of Osiris she is, she was, who walks through the world with his gifts. She carries them burning into her skin, shining out of her body, yes

but her skin is her own, her blood is her own, her pulse, her marrow, her atoms. Great chain of matter, creaturely **Fera**, running through cells, saying now, here, you, this only, this body, breath on this earth now, asking what is this, this *she*, this marriage, this thought of divisions? Running beyond, casting off, proliferating, you, now, here: **Fera the blood heat Fera the cut skin Fera the shit Fera the piss Fera the cum Fera the vomit Fera the snot Fera the veins Fera the arteries Fera the spit Fera the cells Fera the rot Fera the birth Fera decay Fera the kill Fera**

saying now, here, you, this only, this body, breath on this earth now. Claim you.

She breaks through to a town square and onto a beach or a dock or a harbour and there is the sea, and the moon, vivid breaking-upon of the moon in the night air, breaking upon the sea's stillness and she runs towards the froth of the shore, wades, reaches forwards her hands to swim, to be in the sea which is also to be with the moon and the sky, this gentle dark and hazy light, this warm clean air, this feeling of openness and lightness, all heaviness, all grit, gone.

To swim is hard, to keep swimming, away from the town and the rows of electric lamps, but it is better, anything is better, than feeling nothing, touching nothing. It is better than hiding in brush and long grass, flinching from being seen all the time, better than being hobbled again. It is better even than all her stunned and beautiful ascending, for it is the work, here before her as the current swells: the breath, the creaturely pulse, the limbs moving. Swim.

ACKNOWLEDGEMENTS

My thanks to Jess Chandler of prototype press for including an extract from *Wife of Osiris* in *prototype 2* (2020). THANK YOU, Stuart Bartholomew and the team at Verve Poetry Press, for giving *Wife of Osiris* a home and being a joy to work with. Lastly, huge thanks to Richard Dunn for his support when the *Wife &* I needed to be alone.

Any profit I make personally from the sale of this pamphlet will be donated to Rape Crisis and the International Committee of the Red Cross.

ABOUT THE AUTHOR

Meryl Pugh lives in East London and teaches for Poetry School and University of East Anglia. She is the author of two previous pamphlets, *The Bridle* (2011, Salt) and *Relinquish* (2007, Arrowhead), as well as one full collection. *Natural Phenomena* (2018, Penned-in-the-Margins) was the Poetry Book Society's 2018 Spring Guest Choice, a Poetry School Book of the Year and long-listed for the 2020 Laurel Prize. She is currently writing *Feral City*, a work of creative non-fiction, due out from Penned-in-the-Margins in 2022.

ABOUT VERVE POETRY PRESS

Verve Poetry Press is a quite new and already award-winning press that focused initially on meeting a local need in Birmingham - a need for the vibrant poetry scene here in Brum to find a way to present itself to the poetry world via publication. Co-founded by Stuart Bartholomew and Amerah Saleh, it now publishes poets from all corners of the UK and beyond - poets that speak to the city's varied and energetic qualities and will contribute to its many poetic stories.

Added to this is a colourful pamphlet series, many featuring poets who have performed at our sister festival - and a poetry show series which captures the magic of longer poetry performance pieces by festival alumni such as Polarbear, Matt Abbott and Genevieve Carver.

In 2019 the press was voted Most Innovative Publisher at the Saboteur Awards, and won the Publisher's Award for Poetry Pamphlets at the Michael Marks Awards.

Like the festival, we strive to think about poetry in inclusive ways and embrace the multiplicity of approaches towards this glorious art.

www.vervepoetrypress.com
@VervePoetryPres
mail@vervepoetrypress.com